The History of the Car

Elizabeth Raum

Heinemann
LIBRARY

www.heinemann.co.uk/library
Visit our website to find out more information about Heinemann Library books.

To order:
Phone 44 (0)1865 888066
Send a fax to 44 (0)1865 314091
 Visit the Heinemann Bookshop at www.heinemann.co.uk/library to browse our catalogue and order online.

First published in Great Britain by Heinemann Library,
Halley Court, Jordan Hill, Oxford OX2 8EJ, part of
Pearson Education.
Heinemann is a registered trademark of Pearson
Education Ltd.

Editorial: Kristen Truhlar and Diyan Leake
Design: Victoria Bevan and Tower Designs Ltd
Picture research: Mica Brancic
Production: Julie Carter

Origination: Dot Gradations
Printed and bound in China by South China
Printing Co. Ltd

ISBN 978 0 431 19147 8 (hardback)
12 11 10 09 08
10 9 8 7 6 5 4 3 2 1

ISBN 978 0 431 19153 9 (paperback)
13 12 11 10 09
10 9 8 7 6 5 4 3 2 1

British Library Cataloguing in Publication Data
Raum, Elizabeth
The history of the car. - (Inventions that changed
the world)
1. Automobiles - History - Juvenile literature
2. Automobiles - Social aspects - Juvenile literature
I. Title
303.4'832
ISBN-13: 9780431191539

Acknowledgements
The publishers would like to thank the following for
permission to reproduce photographs: p. 4 The Bridgeman
Art Library/The Fleming-Wyfold Art Foundation, p. 5 Corbis/
Seneca Ray Stoddard, p. 6 Topfoto/Roger-Viollet, p. 7 Science
Photo Library, p. 8 akg-images, p. 9 Rex Features/Roger Viollet,
p. 10 Corbis/Bettman, p. 11 Science & Society/Science Museum,
p. 12 Mary Evans Picture Library, p. 13 Corbis/Bettman,
p. 14 Getty Images/Topical Press Agency, p. 15 Corbis, p. 16
Heritage-Images/National Motor Museum, p. 17 Corbis, p.
18 Rex Features/Pharie/Voisin, p. 19 Alamy/John Powell, p. 20
Corbis/Bettman, p. 21 Getty Images/Collection Mix: Subjects/
Car Culture, p. 22 Royal Dutch Shell, p. 23 Topfoto/The Image
Works, p. 24 Corbis/ZUMA/Toronto Star/David Cooper, p. 25
Getty Images/Science Faction/Peter Ginter, p. 26 Photolibrary.
com/Workbook, Inc/Augustus Butera, p. 27 Getty Images/Stone.

Cover photograph of a Model T Ford from around 1919,
reproduced with permission of Getty/Hulton Archive/Three
Lions.

Every effort has been made to contact copyright holders
of any material reproduced in this book. Any omissions will
be rectified in subsequent printings if notice is given to the
publishers.

Contents

Some words are shown in bold, **like this**. You can find out what they mean by looking in the glossary.

Before cars

Before cars, most people did not travel far from home. They walked to schools and shops. In some places, people rode horses.

Before cars, children walked to school.

Many people used wagons like this one to go places.

People used wagons to carry heavy loads. Some wagons carried people from place to place. Horses pulled the wagons.

The first cars

In 1769 a man from France named Nicholas-Joseph Cugnot made the first **steam** car. A steam car needed a **boiler**, or stove. The boiler made steam to make the car go. The boiler made the steam car heavy.

Nicholas-Joseph Cugnot's steam car was slow.

The Stanley brothers, of the United States, made this steam car. It was fast enough to win a race.

Inventors made better steam cars. Some were very fast. But most people decided that steam cars were too heavy to use every day.

The first motorcars

In 1885 a man from Germany named Karl Benz made the first **motorcar**. His car had an **engine** that used **petrol** instead of **steam**. Benz's motorcar only went as fast as a bicycle.

Karl Benz's motorcar had three wheels instead of four.

In 1886 Gottlieb Daimler built a car with four wheels.

Gottlieb Daimler, who was also from Germany, made a better petrol engine. First he put it on a bicycle to make the first motorcycle. Later on, he put it in a car.

Making and selling cars

Charles and Frank Duryea began work as bike makers in the United States. In 1893 they built their first car. They began to sell cars to other people in 1896. Soon companies in the United States, England, France, Germany, and Italy began making cars to sell.

At first, only people with a lot of money could buy cars.

These cars are all parked in front of a hotel.

At first, not many people bought cars. Cars cost a lot of money and they were noisy. But soon many people wanted cars. By 1900 there were 8,000 cars driving on roads in the United States.

Henry Ford's Model T

In 1903 Henry Ford began the Ford Motor Company in the United States. Ford made a car called the Model T. It seemed as if everyone wanted a Model T.

This photo shows Henry Ford and his son, Edsel, riding in a Ford car.

Cars made on the assembly line all looked alike. These Ford Model Ts were all painted black.

Henry Ford tried something new. It was called an **assembly line**. The assembly line made many Model Ts quickly. By 1927 the Ford Motor Company had made 15 million Model Ts.

Starters and tyres

Early cars were very hard to start. A driver had to turn a **crank** in the front of the car. In 1912 the Cadillac Automobile Company made cars that started with a key. These cars were easier to start.

This man is turning a crank to start his car.

The first car tyres were made of wood. It was bumpy to ride in a car with wooden tyres. In 1904 car companies began to use rubber tyres. Rubber tyres made it easier to ride in cars.

This car has rubber tyres and starts with a key.

Faster and fancier cars

The Model T was a slow car. Some people wanted cars to go fast. They wanted a sports car. Sports cars could not be made on an **assembly line**. Assembly lines made all cars alike, but each sports car was different.

There was no other car just like this 1935 Bugatti race car.

Some people who had a lot of money owned very fancy cars.

Sports cars and **fancy** cars were made one at a time. Fancy cars came in many different colours, and some had extra lights. These cars cost a lot of money. People liked to show off their fancy cars.

Car seats and seat belts

In 1933 the first car seats were **invented**. They were not as safe as today's car seats. The first laws about child safety seats were passed in the United States in 1978. Now in many countries all babies and young children must use car safety seats.

Car seats help keep babies and children safe.

Seat belts keep people safe during car rides.

In 1959 an **inventor** in Sweden named Nils Bohlin came up with the seat belts we use today. Seat belts made it safer to travel by car. In the 1960s, TV and newspaper ads told people that seat belts save lives. Today all cars come with seat belts.

Smaller and bigger cars

In the 1950s and 1960s, cars got smaller. Cars like the Volkswagen from Germany were sold all over the world. Cars cost less and less. More and more people bought them.

Four people could fit inside of a Volkswagen.

Many people can fit inside a people carrier.

In the 1970s and 1980s, car companies made people carriers. They were big enough for a lot of people to fit inside. Most had room for seven or more people.

New kinds of fuel

The first cars used **petrol** to run their **engines**. Most cars still do. Petrol costs a lot of money. It makes the air dirty.

Most cars need to be filled up with petrol to run.

A hybrid car uses less petrol. In the future, cars may not need petrol at all.

Today people are looking for cleaner kinds of **fuel**. Hybrid cars use petrol and **electricity** to run. Hybrid cars use less petrol than other cars. They help keep the air clean.

A world of cars

Today car buyers have many choices.
They can buy a small car for one or two
people. They can buy a car big enough
for the family. They can even buy
a middle-sized car.

Today cars come in
all shapes and sizes.

Inventors are working to make cars safer. The cars of the future will have **automatic** brakes that stop the car before an accident. In the future, cars will be even safer than they are today.

These crash dummies help inventors test new ideas for making cars safer.

How cars changed life

Today cars take us many places. We ride in cars to schools and shops. Very few people ride horses to travel.

Cars are used to carry many things, such as food from the supermarket.

Today cars help people travel to many different places.

People travel far from home. Thanks to cars, we no longer have to stay near home. Cars take us places we have never been before. Cars have changed the way we live.

Timeline

1769 Nicholas-Joseph Cugnot **invents** a **steam** car.

1885 Karl Benz builds a **motorcar**.

1893 Duryea brothers build their first car.

1896 First cars are for sale in the United States.

1903 Ford Motor Company begins work.

1904 Rubber tyres are put on cars.

1912 Cars with keys are invented.

1933 First car seats are for sale.

1959 Nils Bohlin invents the seat belt.

1978 First seat belt laws are passed in the United States.

1997 Hybrid car is invented.

World map activity

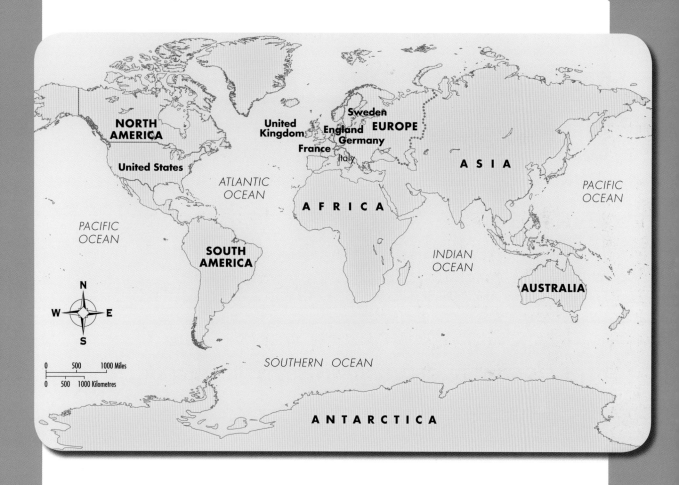

The countries talked about in this book are labelled on this world map. Try to find each **inventor**'s country on the map.

Find out more

Books

All About Cars, Peter Harrison (Southwater, 2003).

Inventing the Automobile, Erinn Banting (Crabtree, 2006).

Cars: The Essential Guide, Simon Jowett (DK Publishing, 2006).

Websites

Enchanted Learning –
http://www.enchantedlearning.com/inventors

Technology at Home –
http://www.pbs.org/wgbh/aso/tryit/tech

PBS – Early Cars
http://pbskids.org/wayback/tech1900/car.html

Glossary

assembly line when each worker does one job, such as putting the tyres on a car

automatic something that can do things without people making it work

boiler stove used in a steam car, train, or ship

crank handle that starts an engine

electricity kind of energy

engine part of a car that makes it go

fancy has extra things that are not needed

fuel something that gives power

invent make something that did not exist before

inventor someone who makes something that did not exist before

motorcar type of car that uses a petrol engine

petrol liquid used to make a car go

steam water turned to gas by heating

Index